Bible Stories that Make Us Smile

Bible Stories that Make Us Smile

TOLD BY
Carolyn Osiek

ILLUSTRATED BY
Patricia Reid

RESOURCE *Publications* • Eugene, Oregon

BIBLE STORIES THAT MAKE US SMILE

Resource Publications
An Imprint of Wipf and Stock Publishers
199 W. 8th Ave., Suite 3
Eugene, OR 97401

www.wipfandstock.com

PAPERBACK ISBN: 978-1-7252-5680-4
HARDCOVER ISBN: 978-1-7252-5681-1
EBOOK ISBN: 978-1-7252-5682-8

Manufactured in the U.S.A.   01/16/20

Contents

Introduction

Dear Reader,

We love these Bible stories that have been told and cherished through so many generations.

As we remembered them, we began to see them from new points of view and with new visual representations. We share these stories with you, in the hope that it will lead you to think about them and tell them again from your own point of view.

Carolyn Osiek, RSCJ*

Patricia Reid, RSCJ*

*The letters "RSCJ" stand for Religious of the Sacred Heart of Jesus in French (*Religieuses du Sacré-Coeur de Jésus*), a Roman Catholic order of religious sisters, founded in France in 1800 and present today in forty countries. www.rscj.org.

1 The Prophets Who Didn't Want to Be

The people of Israel had been slaves in Egypt until God led them out through God's chosen leader, Moses. Moses was God's prophet. That meant that Moses could talk to God and hear and understand what God answered, and tell the people.

They had left Egypt with its palm trees and river Nile and springs of water and plenty of food. Yes, they had been slaves and now they were free. But now they were camped out in the desert, hot, dry, and boring. Nothing to do and nothing to eat, either. So they complained to the man in charge, Moses, who complained to God who had put him in that situation in the first place.

God had to do something to save face and so they would know that God was still in charge. So God told Moses to choose seventy leaders from the people, and God would take some of the prophetic spirit from Moses and share it with them, so they could help Moses with his work and he wouldn't have to be leader of all the people alone. Moses thought that sounded like a good idea, so he called the seventy leaders to go out of the camp with him to God's favorite place to meet with him, not very far away.

Somehow, the message about when to leave with Moses didn't get through to two of these leaders, Eldad and Medad. They got their part of the prophetic spirit all right, that was for sure. But it made them pretty tired, and they slept in too long that morning. By the time they woke up, the whole group had left them behind! They were pretty worried about what would happen, but God didn't seem to notice. God just went ahead and made the other leaders outside the camp prophesy—and Eldad and Medad did, too, even though they were still at home. Just like the others, they were filled with joy and excitement, and began to say to the people around them what God wanted them to say.

But it seems that wherever you go, there are tattle tales. One boy saw them acting like prophets at home, when he knew they were supposed to be outside with the others. So he had nothing better to do than to run out to Moses and tell him about Eldad and Medad acting like prophets at home when they were supposed to be out there with the others. Moses had an assistant, Joshua, who thought that this was out of order and just had to stop. "Moses, stop them!" he cried. But Moses didn't think that was the thing to do. Instead, he said that being a prophet was such a good thing that he wished all God's people would be able to be prophets.

Moses understood more about what God is like than any of the others did. Even if we don't make it to the right place at the right time, God still loves us and won't give up on us.

Numbers 11:24–30

2 The Angel and the Donkey

Long ago, there were people called the Moabites who lived near the Jordan River. Another people, the nation of Israel, were immigrants, moving from Egypt through the land of the Moabites, who were afraid of the Israelites because there were so many of them. Their king Balak sent a message to Balaam, a prophet who lived nearby, to come and curse the Israelites. That means he would say bad things about them so that God would make bad things happen to them and they would not prosper. This way his people would not feel so threatened by them. Prophets were supposed to do things like this, and people believed that they had the power to make God listen and do what they wanted.

Balaam was ready to take the job, but God told him to knock it off because the Israelites were God's special friends, and God didn't want bad things to happen to them. But King Balak of the Moabites wouldn't take no for an answer. Balaam had the reputation of being the best prophet around, and he wanted only the best. He kept insisting so much that finally Balaam gave in and said yes.

The prophet saddled his donkey and set out, with two servants to help him. But God didn't like this idea, because the people he was supposed to curse were Israel and God was on their side. So God told an angel to hurry down there, go ahead of the prophet, and stand in the way on the road to stop him. The angel did, and the donkey stopped in her tracks—because the angel looked really scary and held a sword in his hand!

The donkey was so scared that she turned off the road into the nearby field. The trouble was that only the donkey could see the angel. Balaam, even though he was a prophet and was supposed to see things that other people couldn't see, could not see the angel.

"Whoa! I want nothing to do with you," said the donkey to the angel. "That's smart of you," said the angel.

But Balaam didn't know why the donkey was behaving like that because he couldn't see the angel, so he beat the poor donkey and made her get back on the road. By that time, the angel was gone. So they went a little farther, and there was the angel again, in a narrow part of the road with vineyards on either side, so the donkey couldn't get through. This time she squeezed against the wall and scraped Balaam's foot on it. This time Balaam was really angry, and beat the donkey, but when she looked up, the angel had disappeared again. Still, only the donkey could see the angel.

2 THE ANGEL AND THE DONKEY

They went on a little farther and came to a place where there was a high wall of rock on either side of the road, and there was the angel again, blocking the way. There was nothing for the poor donkey to do but lie down under Balaam, right there on the road. For the third time, Balaam beat the donkey. He was so angry with the donkey that he said if he had a sword, he would kill her. It was a good thing he didn't have a sword! The donkey started talking to him right there, and said, "Why are you beating me? Haven't I always done just what you wanted me to do?" Balaam agreed that up to this time, she had been a very well-behaved donkey.

"Ok, this has gone far enough," said the donkey. "What's going on? Why can't the prophet see you, too, angel?"

"Oh!" said the angel. "This contraption I have is new. I'm not sure how to use it. It controls who can see me, and I turned on my animal-view switch but I forgot to turn on my people-view switch, so people can see me. Sorry." Of course, if the angel had had a smartphone, he could have done it with just a click—but they didn't have smartphones then.

So the angel turned on his people-view switch, too. The prophet saw the angel and apologized to his donkey. He definitely got the idea that God didn't want him to go on, so he was ready to turn around and go back home.

The story goes on from there, though. By that time, he was so far from home that God told him to go on. Balaam was supposed to curse Israel but as it turned out, just the opposite happened: the prophet had to say what God wanted him to say. Instead of cursing Israel, he blessed them and said all kinds of good things about them.

Be careful when your pet animal doesn't want to go with you the way you want it to go. Maybe it sees an angel that you can't see!

And sometimes when new people come into the neighborhood, we're afraid of them. But maybe they had a really hard time where they came from, and they are just looking for a place to be happy.

Numbers 22:7–34

3 Being Part of the Family

The people were coming back! Little Sarah was only seven years old, and she belonged to one of the families who had traveled a very long distance. They traveled for months, she, her parents, and her younger brother Jacob. It seemed like they were on the road forever. She wasn't sure where they were going, except that her parents said they were going *home*. It certainly wasn't to the home she knew. That was in the great city of Babylon, where she and her parents and her parents' parents had lived. She knew that they always talked about somewhere else as their real home, but she thought it was just talk, the way the old-timers did, remembering things that happened way before her time.

But now they really had traveled all this distance to another country that they called Israel. She knew that all her family and friends said they were Israelites, so if this was Israel, it must be home. But it wasn't like any home she had known before. They settled in the country, in a small village where her father and her uncles began to farm. At first they didn't know much about farming, but they were learning. They were so happy to be back in what they called their own land. "Well," she thought, "I guess I should be happy, too, but I haven't made any friends here yet, and it's all so new."

Then came the day when they all packed up and traveled again, this time not so far, only for one day. They arrived at a new city where things were being built everywhere you looked. They called it Jerusalem. At one side there was a very impressive building half-built, surrounded by a courtyard. She was told that this was the Temple. She wasn't quite sure what that was, but everyone was giving it special attention. People of all kinds were coming to it, bringing things, especially building materials like wood and stone, but also a lot of gold and silver, and some beautiful robes made with very expensive materials.

She went with her family to one of the gates of the courtyard, and she saw that a great crowd was gathered there, of men, women, and children. Then some women were going through the crowd announcing that the children who were too young would be gathered together in another place for their own play time together, while the grownups listened to what was coming. But if any children were old enough to understand, they could stay.

Sarah looked around, and saw all the younger children trooping along to go and play, even some who looked about her age. But Sarah became very serious and very determined. She would stay! Her parents looked doubtful. Her younger brother Jacob went happily off with the other children. She was urged to go. But she would not go. "I am old enough," she insisted. So her parents let her stay.

A dignified-looking man walked up on a platform where he could see the whole group gathered below. Sarah was told this was Ezra the priest. With him were many other men, thirteen in all. But Ezra was the one who spoke. He began to read from a scroll that he called the Book of the Law. Sarah wasn't sure what that was, but after he read a passage, he would stop and explain it in his own words, so that everybody could understand. She began to get the idea after a while.

This was the word of God telling the people how they should live in their new homeland. At the end, Ezra told them to go and celebrate, because this was a time of rejoicing.

The family picked up Jacob from the children's group and went back to where they were staying in Jerusalem. They had a great party with their friends, and Sarah felt like a grownup. She was now really part of the family!

Nehemiah 8:1–12

4 Coming Home

Ages and ages ago, when there were no kings or queens in Israel, men and even women who were called "judges" ruled in the land. There was a great shortage of food in the city of Bethlehem—nobody was sure where their next meal would come from. So a man there named Elimelech was so worried that his family would have enough to eat that he did what so many people still have to do now. He and his family became refugees. That means they left home not because they wanted to, but because they had to. Elimelech and his wife Naomi and their two sons Mahlon and Chilion had to leave their home and friends and move to another place across the river called the Plains of Moab. (That means the place was really flat!)

The new place became home for them, and they lived there happily for about ten years. Then Elimelech died, leaving his wife Naomi alone with their sons Mahlon and Chilion, who now really wanted to get married since they were grown up. So they each met and fell in love with nice Moabite girls. One was named Orpah and the other one was called Ruth. Unfortunately neither couple had any children, and now that the sons had wives from Moab, they didn't want to go back home to Bethlehem where they were born.

But after another ten years, both Mahlon and Chilion died, leaving their mother Naomi alone. Then Naomi found out that God had given food to the people of her hometown of Bethlehem, so she decided to pack up and leave the Plains of Moab. She didn't like seeing her two daughters-in-law without husbands, so here's what she said: "Go back, each of you to your mother's house. God will find you good new husbands, the way God found you, who were such good wives for my sons. I hope God will make each of you very happy with a new husband."

As they went on their way, Orpah changed her name (Have you ever done that?) and decided to go back to her own people. Naomi kissed them both and that made them cry because they really loved her and didn't want to leave her all alone in a foreign country. But Naomi said: "I'm too old to get married again and to have sons who could marry you!" So Orpah kissed her mother-in-law and went back to her own people.

But Ruth wouldn't leave Naomi. She insisted on staying with her and told her: "Don't make me leave you. Wherever you go, I want to go, too, and wherever you live, I want to live. Your people will be my people and your God will be my God, too." The Moabites didn't worship the God of Israel, so she was even willing to change her religion for the sake of her mother-in-law, Naomi.

When Naomi realized that Ruth wasn't going to change her mind, she gave in. Although it had been twenty years since Naomi had left her home town of Bethlehem, she said it was time to go back. So the two of them set out, Naomi to return to the home she had left long ago and Ruth to go to a new land where she had never been, with a different language and customs, out of love for her mother-in-law Naomi. They arrived in Bethlehem at the beginning of the barley harvest, in the early spring.

Naomi had a rich cousin named Boaz. Ruth told her, "I'd like to go into the fields and pick up some ears of barley that the harvesters leave behind. Maybe the owner of the field will like me." Naomi thought that was a good idea. This was a custom in Israel. The harvest was all done by hand, not by big machines the way they do it today, and the harvesters were supposed to not go back to pick up anything they didn't get the first time around, so the poor people could come and take it.

So Ruth went out to collect some wheat left by the reapers. By good luck (or maybe God planned it this way) Boaz noticed Ruth, so he asked one of the reapers who she was. The reaper replied, "That's the girl from Moab who came back with Naomi."

Boaz seemed really interested in Ruth, so he said to her, "Listen, my daughter (he called her that because she looked so young), you mustn't work in any other field but mine." He was very kind to her and warned his workers not to annoy her. He even invited her to drink from the workers' water pitchers.

Boaz was super kind to Ruth partly because he had learned about her husband's death and about her kindness to her mother-in-law, Naomi. Boaz was really impressed with her goodness and Ruth was very grateful for his kindness.

Naomi decided it was time for Ruth to settle down and get married again, and because Boaz was a close relative to Naomi, she agreed that it was a good idea for him to marry Ruth. She had been like a true daughter to Naomi. So Boaz decided to marry Ruth and soon they became parents. Their firstborn son was Obed, who later grew up to become the father of Jesse, who was the father of King David. That made Ruth King David's great-grandmother. The family tree continues after David for several centuries until it comes to Mary and Joseph of Nazareth, whose son was Jesus, born in the same little town of Bethlehem.

The book of Ruth. Read the whole story.

5 A Very Big Fish Story

Hello. My name is Dag, but you can call me Doug. That's probably easier for you to remember. I'm a fish. A big fish. A *very big* fish. Big enough to swallow a person—but I'm getting ahead of my story. Later, some people who told my story called me a whale. Well, a whale *looks like* a very big fish, but in fact, a whale is not a fish. More on that later.

My home is in the sea not far from the coast of Israel. I have a good time swimming around and enjoying the water because it isn't too cold there. I don't usually meet any people, since they aren't swimming as far out or as deep as where I live. I don't usually get direct messages from God either, but one day I did.

There was a terrible storm up on the surface of the water. Storms don't really affect us fish, because we just go deeper into the water until we find a depth where it's completely calm. When I looked up that day, I could see way above me that it was a pretty bad storm. Then all of a sudden, the storm stopped.

There was a man named Jonah who had just been thrown off a boat by the crew because they believed *he* was the cause of the storm! And they were right. God was angry with him for not doing what God had commanded him, and as soon as they threw him into the sea, the storm stopped. That was when I got a message from God. It was God's voice telling me in no uncertain terms what I was supposed to do: go up and swallow Jonah! Well, I always do what God tells me to do—it's a good idea to do that. So without even an introduction, I just jumped up and swallowed poor Jonah.

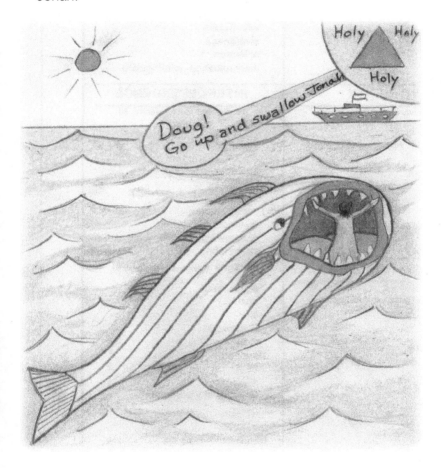

I guess he was pretty surprised. While he was inside me, I could hear him praying out loud, but there was no way I could talk to him. He stayed there for three days while I swam around. I started getting pretty hungry, because I couldn't eat anything else while he was inside—he was taking up all the space in my stomach.

Finally, after three days, God spoke to me again and said it was time to get rid of him, but I should put him out on dry land. That wasn't easy. I had to find a place where it was shallow enough that he could wade to shore, but deep enough where I could still get back in the water and go home. It took some searching but I did find a place, and it turned out to be very close to where he had gotten on that boat in the first place.

As I learned later, when Jonah got on that boat, he was going in the opposite direction from where God wanted him to go. After all that, he got the message and went to Nineveh, where God wanted him. Nineveh is very far inland, so I've never been there and have no intention of ever going there. But this is an important thing to learn, isn't it: it doesn't work to run away from God.

My story was so good that people kept telling it, and writing songs about it, and painting pictures of me—but most of these people had never seen a fish as big as I am, so they imagined me in many different ways. Some of them knew about whales, that are really mammals that breathe air but live in the ocean, and they thought that's what I am. Others imagined me as some sort of sea monster, more like a big snake than a big fish. I don't really like being called a different species than I am. I'm a fish, but I suppose calling me something else makes for a good story.

Well, I've had enough of all this popularity because I'm rather shy. I'm going back to my home deep in the ocean and you can go on telling your stories about me but you won't see me. Bye bye.

The book of Jonah. You can read the whole story.

Note for grownups: In the original Hebrew text, the creature that swallows Jonah is a *dag gadol*, just a "big fish," not a whale and not a sea monster. There are whales in the Mediterranean Sea, and seafarers had probably seen them but not realized that they are in fact mammals.

6 It's a Bird, It's a Plane —It's Habakkuk!

Once in Babylon a long time ago, a young man named Daniel was in big trouble. It was decided in the king's court that no other god could be worshiped except the king himself. But Daniel continued to pray to his own God, the God of Israel. As punishment, Daniel was thrown into a den of lions and left there, to see if his God would deliver him or if he would be killed and eaten by the lions.

Meanwhile, it was a pretty quiet day far away in Judea. It was harvest time, and the workers were out in the field, working in the hot sun all morning to harvest the grain so they could make bread to enjoy all year. In those days, they didn't have big farm machines to do it fast as it's done in some places today. But still today, there are many places where the harvest is done by hand. In our story, there were men, women, and children, whole families out there in the heat working from sunup, working by hand. It was almost lunch time and they were all getting pretty hungry.

There was a man named Habakkuk whose job it was to bring them their lunch in the field. He got it ready, a great meat stew with bread, and was heading out to deliver it, when all of a sudden, he saw an angel standing in front of him! It was a big angel, bigger than Habakkuk, the kind of guy you don't want to mess with. He had a message for Habakkuk, in fact, it was a command: "Never mind all those hungry workers out there. Take that food to Daniel in the lions' den in Babylon."

Now, Babylon was very far away. Habakkuk said he had never been there, didn't know where it was, and didn't know anything about any lions' den. He figured that would be enough to convince the angel that he had the wrong man for the job. But the angel thought, well, the saying is true, all right: if you want something done, you have to do it yourself. Without another word, he picked up Habakkuk by the hair and flew him lickety-split to Babylon! The workers in the field looked up at something zipping along in the sky and they weren't sure what it was, but Habakkuk was gone and so was the pot of stew! So much for lunch.

In a quick moment, Habakkuk and the angel were in Babylon. Any other time, it would have taken months to get there, but angels can do it right away. The angel set Habakkuk down at the edge of the lions' den, so neatly that he landed on his feet, even holding the big pot of stew. Habakkuk saw a young man sitting there, looking a little confused, surrounded by several lions that looked even more confused, and he figured that must be Daniel. "Here's your lunch," Habakkuk said, and carefully—very carefully— let it down to Daniel, keeping an eye on all those lions. But the lions didn't seem interested in the lunch, or in having Daniel or Habakkuk for lunch. Daniel thanked Habakkuk and thanked God for bringing him something to eat.

Before he knew it, Habakkuk was back home in the field near his house in Judea, once again having flown through the air in an instant, carried by the angel holding him by his hair. On the way back, Habakkuk was kind of getting the hang of it and thinking, "Wow! I'm flying!" But he only had time to think of it once, and he was back where he started. The difference was, this time no lunch for the workers. All those hungry workers were now staring at him, not at all happy. They weren't impressed by the flying trick and now they had to go hungry.

It was a good thing that Habakkuk's wife had seen the whole thing. She ran back to the kitchen and started making another stew for the workers. It wasn't quite as much as the first one, but it was better than nothing. So the workers had something to eat and Daniel back there in Babylon was quite well fed, and ready to meet the king when he came back to see how Daniel was.

In the end, the only one who wasn't happy at all was Habakkuk's barber, who had quite a time getting all those tangles out of Habakkuk's hair.

Daniel 14:33–39. You might not be able to find this story in your Bible. It depends on what kind of Bible you have. It's in what some people call the Apocrypha or the Additions to Daniel. But it has been part of the story of Daniel for a very long time.

7 The Angel Who Sat on the Stone

It was very early on Easter morning. Dawn was just beginning. Heather, one of the lower angels, was enjoying some free time on a particularly lovely cloud. Suddenly, her angel supervisor was looking for her frantically. "Quick," he said. "We need you down on earth." The angel who was assigned to a very important job got called away to solve an urgent problem in Babylon.

7 THE ANGEL WHO SAT ON THE STONE

Heather was not a very important angel, and she had never been given an important job before, so she was surprised. Her assignment was to go to a garden outside Jerusalem, roll back the stone of a tomb, and greet Jesus as he rose from the tomb! She had to practice first and get the approval of her supervisor. She pushed on the big stone, way bigger than she was, but of course, she was an angel, so she could move it without much trouble.

Once it was rolled out of the way, she just couldn't resist propping herself up and sitting on top of it. She crossed her legs and swung her foot back and forth. What fun! Well, her supervisor wasn't too happy about that, and thought it would be better if she didn't cross her legs and swing her foot. It wasn't dignified for an angel to be so laid back. Heather knew this was a very important assignment, so she promised she would try to remember. Now she was ready. Of course, there is no time with angels, so she didn't really have to hurry to be ready in time. She appeared right on cue, rolled back the stone with a flourish, said hello to Jesus as he came out of the tomb, and hopped up on the stone. But then, she forgot that she wasn't supposed to cross her legs and swing her foot. She just did it anyway!

That was when she noticed the two women standing there outside the tomb, petrified with fear. How had she not noticed them right away? Because she was an angel, when the humans saw her, she was surrounded with bright light — an awesome sight. She wanted to reassure them, so she quickly said "Don't be afraid!" The two women, Mary Magdalene and another named Mary, looked up, shielding their eyes from the bright light that came from Heather, and then they saw a very friendly-looking angel relaxing on top of the stone. "How could we be afraid of an angel who swings her foot like that?" they wondered. Heather told them the good news of Jesus' resurrection, and it made them very happy.

As she was going back to heaven, Heather thought her supervisor angel might be angry with her because she had forgotten to behave in a more dignified way and not swing her foot. But when she got there, she found that everyone in heaven was very happy with her because she had helped the women at the tomb not to be afraid. Instead, they were full of happiness because Jesus was with them again.

Matthew 28:1–8

Note for grownups.

Have you noticed that when Mark tells the story, he sends an angel who disguises himself as a human, who sits *inside* the tomb; he isn't relaxed enough to come out. His attempt to reassure the women doesn't work very well. After they hear what he has to say, they run away *because they were afraid.* Matthew's angel is much better at it, comfortable enough to come out and sit on the stone.

8 Counting for Jesus

Little Jacob was only seven years old, but he loved being with his father and uncles when they went out on their fishing boats in Galilee from their home in Bethsaida, right on the lake. They would go out really early in the morning, before dawn. It wasn't easy for Jacob to get up so early, but he really wanted to be part of the family business, so when his father called him to get up, he would yawn a little, sometimes even roll over again, but on the second call, he was up right away.

After a quick breakfast of bread and cheese, they set out in their boats, dragging their nets, hoping to bring in enough fish that they didn't have to work all day. When Jacob was not out in the fishing boats with the men of the family, he was in school with the village rabbi, learning to read the Bible in Hebrew, which was a lot like his own language, but not quite, and learning to use numbers to add, subtract, and multiply, a skill that was useful in all kinds of business, including counting the fish caught each day and selling them to customers on the shore. Math was his favorite part of school. He even arranged things at home, just for fun, in groups of the same number. For example, when his mother asked him to bring some olives from the olive bin for her cooking, he would first set them out in piles of fifty or a hundred at a time, so that he practiced his counting skills.

Everyone in the village knew about a famous preacher and healer who had been around recently. His name was Jesus and he was from Nazareth, a town about a day's walk from Bethsaida. One day when Jacob and his father and uncles were out in their fishing boat, they looked out over the water and saw a boat that looked familiar, with a lot of men in it. As they got closer, sure enough, it was Jesus and his friends in the boat owned by the Zebedee Brothers, heading in the other direction. But in a few minutes, other fishermen in other boats saw them, too, and started heading in the same direction. They all wanted to hear more from Jesus! Jacob's father and uncles decided to go, too.

So Jesus and his friends landed on a quiet piece of the shore, and it wasn't long before all the other boats landed, too, and there were even people coming out from other villages nearby. It got to be a pretty big crowd. So instead of having what he had hoped was a quiet time with his friends, Jesus looked around at all these guys and felt sorry for them. He began to talk to them, and talked, and talked, and talked. After many hours, his friends were getting anxious. It was late in the day, they hadn't eaten, and they tried to get Jesus to stop talking and make all these guys go home. Instead, Jesus insisted that *they*, his friends, should feed them all, with—are you ready for this? Five loaves of bread and two fish! No way would that work.

It was early spring after some good winter rain, and the grass was fresh and lovely, as it would only be for another month or so before the sun dried it up. It was late afternoon, and the sun was at such an angle that it made beautiful golden shadows among the rocks. Jacob heard Jesus and his friends, and saw the look of terror on their faces. How could they possibly do this? Jacob knew that if the men were arranged neatly in groups, it would be a lot easier to figure out how much food was needed to feed them. So he stepped up and got Jesus' attention. He offered to arrange the crowd in groups of fifty and a hundred and explained why he wanted to do this. Jesus thought it was a good idea. It was pretty unusual to see a little boy telling all these men what to do, but Jesus was there to encourage him.

When they were all arranged, Jacob was right there when Jesus took the bread and fish, blessed it, and told his friends to distribute it. He watched in amazement how the baskets just never got empty. Everybody had something to eat, and at the end, there was more than they had started with: twelve baskets of pieces left over!

They returned home very late that day. It was already dark. His mother was worried because they never stayed out on the lake that late, but she hoped Jacob was safe with his father and uncles, wherever they were. What a story he had to tell her! And even though she was ready to cook for them, they weren't hungry.

Mark 6:30–44

Note for grownups:

Mark's account of the story has some unusual extra details. He is the only one who says the men sat in organized groups, like members of a symposium. At the end, Mark 6:44 specifically says there were five thousand *men*. Matthew worries about that, and adds to the five thousand men, "besides women and children," (Matthew 14:21), but Mark doesn't seem interested in the women and children, just the men. Were there also women and children? Maybe they all came from work, and so were mostly men—except for Jacob, of course.

Evidence indicates that the spoken language in Galilee at the time of Jesus was Aramaic, a language very similar to Hebrew, that had been introduced centuries earlier by foreign invaders. Hebrew was probably spoken by some educated people and kept alive through reading of the Bible.

9 The Sheep Who Wasn't Lost

Hannah was a happy sheep in what she thought was the best flock in the land. They had good pasture, a lovely stream to drink from, and a shepherd who really cared about them. They were a medium-sized flock of about a hundred, small enough that everyone got to know each other at least a little. Of course, some sheep were better friends than others, and the friends usually spent more time together on one particular patch of grass. In Hannah's circle of friends there were about eight, give or take one or two who tended to drift in and out. Most of the others in her circle considered themselves best friends. They would spend some time each day, in the heat of the afternoon, in whatever shade they could find under rocks or trees, lying down and exchanging the news of the day—which wasn't much. Sheep generally do the same thing every day. So the conversation usually lapsed into a pleasant afternoon nap.

There was just one problem in Hannah's circle of sheep friends. It was Rachel. Rachel was a very attractive sheep — well, to other sheep, anyway, and to the shepherd, who tended to treat her with special attention. At least, that's the way in seemed to Hannah, who would have liked some of the special attention herself. Maybe the reason the shepherd watched her closely was that she had a tendency to wander off a little, all by herself, to the point that Hannah considered it dangerous. There were all kinds of dangers out there: wolves, thieves, everything a sheep could imagine.

One day it happened, what Hannah was afraid would happen. Rachel wandered off so far that she got left behind. What was it she was following? Who knows, but she was gone. Hannah and her friends looked frantic enough that the shepherd noticed their distress. Because he knew Rachel so well, he realized quickly that she was missing. To be honest, Hannah was not so much afraid as annoyed. What was wrong with Rachel that she did this? Didn't she know how much distress it caused her friends? Didn't she realize the extra work that their shepherd would have to put in to find her—IF he could find her before the wolves did?

Now this was a big risk for the shepherd if he wanted to go after her. What about all the others? He was alone and couldn't get anyone to watch them while he went away. But he took a deep breath and set out looking for Rachel. The word had spread quickly in the flock and everyone knew she was missing. When they saw the shepherd set out, they knew what to do. They bunched together so tightly that it would have been pretty hard for wolves to attack. They would get a taste of heels kicking at them. Besides, it was the middle of the day so the chance of a wolf attack was not as serious as if it had been at twilight.

Happily, it didn't take too long before the shepherd found her, terrified, walking in circles bleating "Help!" in Sheep language. The shepherd didn't speak Sheep but he got the idea pretty fast anyway. Before she could protest, he swept her up and put her around his shoulders for the walk back to the flock.

When they returned, all the sheep relaxed and breathed a sigh of relief. Rachel was looking very—well, sheepish. Hannah was still annoyed at her. By this time, it was time to go home for the day. When they got home to the sheep pen, Hannah saw the shepherd talking to his neighbors about what happened and how they should all be happy with him because he found his lost sheep. Hannah thought this was really too much. Rachel shouldn't be getting all that attention. Rachel heard it, too, and batted her eyelashes coyly so the neighbors would know that *she* was the sheep that the shepherd loved so much that he put all the others at risk to find. That made Hannah even more annoyed.

To make things even worse, the neighbors were all together because they had a visitor, a man named Jesus from Nazareth. He was telling stories, and all the people, and those sheep who could get close enough, were listening. Someone asked him what he had to say to the complaint about him, that he welcomed sinners and even ate meals with them. In answer, he told them to think about what they had just heard from the shepherd about finding his lost sheep. Now Hannah was really annoyed. Comparing sinners to sheep? Sheep are not sinners! They try to be the best sheep they can be. But maybe, Hannah thought, sometimes people act like sheep, wandering off where they shouldn't go like Rachel, or not sticking together when they should.

As Hannah was thinking about all this, she must have looked pretty confused. Then she noticed a hand coming down on her head. It was the visitor, Jesus, who saw how upset she was and laid his hand gently on her head to calm her. Well, that made her day, and she forgot all about her annoyance at Rachel. All she could think of was how she wanted to be a really good sheep, because she knew that Jesus really loved her just as much as Rachel.

Luke 15:1–7; Matthew 18:12–14

10 Up a Tree

Zacchaeus was a rich man. The reason he was so rich was that he was a tax collector. It wasn't like today, when grown-ups have to mail in their taxes to the government or send them online. These tax collectors went out and took the tax money from people, and turned it in to the government, which paid them for their services. Everybody thought they were crooks because they charged too much and kept the difference. So they weren't the favorite people in town. But they worked for the government so you had to be careful not to get them mad at you.

Zacchaeus did his tax collecting work in Jericho, which was a big, rich city. He had plenty of work and so plenty of money. He even had other tax collectors working for him, because collecting the taxes in Jericho was too big a job for one man. Life was pretty good except that he wasn't very popular, for good reason, so he didn't have many friends. There was one other thing: Zacchaeus was short. Sometimes people don't take short people very seriously, if they can tower over them and look powerful. It was pretty hard when Zacchaeus had to convince some tall rich guy that he really did owe this much tax, and he'd better cough it up or get in trouble.

Just about everybody in town heard the news: Jesus of Nazareth was headed this way! By now he was pretty well known, and crowds turned out just to see him and hope he would say something inspiring. The crowd was already forming when Zacchaeus got up from his desk, and he could see that he wasn't going to be able to see anything over all those people, so he went outside and had an idea: he was still limber enough to climb the tree right outside his house. So he did, and from there, he could see Jesus coming along the street.

Zacchaeus, come down!

What happened next was a total surprise. Jesus stopped at the tree, looked up, and spoke to Zacchaeus. Jesus even knew his name without asking! And everybody standing around heard it. They wondered why Zacchaeus was up a tree and why Jesus was paying attention to this guy they would rather not have around, especially up in a tree. That Jesus was even talking to Zacchaeus was a mystery, and then what he said really topped it off: Jesus said he wanted to stay at Zacchaeus' house!

Well, Zacchaeus had a very nice guest room, with a view even, but nobody except other tax collectors ever stayed there because they wouldn't want to be seen associating with Zacchaeus. Jesus didn't seem to mind all that. He wanted to reach out to Zacchaeus to say, even you can be loved by God.

Zacchaeus scrambled back down the tree, and he looked pretty funny by the time he got halfway down, with all his neighbors watching and laughing. But he kept coming down because he had something to say, too. We don't know whether what he said next was true or whether he was making it up as he went along. He made himself sound like a pretty good guy. He said that he gave half of his riches to the poor, and that if he found out that he had cheated somebody, he paid back four times the amount. What we don't know is whether he really was doing that already or had just made up his mind that from then on, that's what he would do.

In any case, it made Jesus happy because everybody else thought of Zacchaeus as a lost cause, but Jesus saw the good in him, the way he does with everybody.

Luke 19:1–10

11 Left Out in the Cold

Just a few years after the time of Jesus, there was an important lady in Jerusalem named Mary—no relation to the mother of Jesus, who also had the same name. This Mary had a large house and many servants. She also had a son named John Mark, who later became a companion of St. Paul. But her son John Mark is not part of this story.

In Mary's house there was a door maid named Rose. She was good at her job, making sure the entrance to the house was clean and tidy, and she was careful only to let in the right people when they knocked, day or night. But Rose had one problem: she was afraid of ghosts. Sometimes she had terrible nightmares about scary ghosts coming after her, and she was very much afraid of walking around the house alone at night.

One day one of their dear friends, St. Peter, was arrested and thrown into jail because he kept talking about Jesus when the people around him didn't want him to. They wanted to be sure Peter couldn't escape, so they had him in chains between two guards, with more guards at the door. But God had other ideas and sent an angel to spring him out of jail late one night. They were all asleep, guards and Peter, too. Suddenly he felt somebody pushing him on his side. He opened his eyes and saw the angel, who told him to get up and get dressed with his belt and sandals and coat, to get ready to travel.

Together they went past all the guards, and the big heavy gate of the prison opened by itself. Peter of course thought he was dreaming, until he found himself, very much awake, on the street outside. So there he was on the street in the middle of the night. The angel was no help. She hit the road as soon as she had done her job of getting him out of jail. Where could Peter go? He remembered his friend Mary and knew someone would be up at her house—and he was right. All his friends were there together praying for him, thinking he was still in jail, praying and hoping that nothing bad would happen to him. So he made his way down the dark, empty streets until he found the front door of Mary's house. He knocked on the door. It was Rose's job to open the door, day or night. She was really afraid because she didn't know who would be knocking in the middle of the night. Maybe it was somebody scary, who shouldn't be let in. But the knocking continued, so she took a deep breath and opened the door. She couldn't believe her eyes. There was Peter looking back at her.

"Well, aren't you going to let me in?" he asked. "Oh no!" she thought. It can't be Peter—he's in jail. Peter must have died, and this is his ghost. I have to keep him out!" So she slammed the door in his face, leaving poor Peter standing outside in the street. Rose ran back to tell the others that there was a ghost outside who looked just like Peter. A lot of the people inside thought the same thing, that Peter was dead and it must be Peter's ghost at the door.

It was a good thing that Mary didn't believe in ghosts. If she did, Peter might still be out there knocking on the door. She quickly ran to the door and brought Peter inside. Everyone was amazed to see him. He sat down in a warm place near the fire and they brought him some food and a hot drink. All his friends sat around him.

He told them how God had worked a miracle to get him out of jail. Rose sat there listening along with the others. At one point, Peter looked at her, smiled, and laid his hand on her head in blessing. From that day on, Rose was no longer afraid of ghosts.

Acts 12:12–17

12 Don't Mess with Jesus or Paul

Paul was traveling around everywhere teaching people the good news about Jesus and how he would save them from their sins if they believed in him. He was having a lot of success, but he noticed that there were lots of people who needed more than just words. They were sick and wounded, and of course, there were no clinics or hospitals for them. Paul wanted to be able to heal these people the way Jesus did in Galilee and Jerusalem. Paul was far away from there. He was in a big city called Ephesus that was about a month's travel away.

Because Paul wanted to heal these people, God gave him special powers to show how strong Jesus is and how much he wants to heal sick people. Paul would call on Jesus' name to heal people, and they got better. There were many people who were sick and behaving very strangely, so that the people thought that evil spirits had entered into them that had to be chased out. Because of what God did for Paul, his power to heal was so strong that all sick people had to do was touch him or even touch a piece of cloth that had touched him and they would get well.

There were seven brothers there in Ephesus who watched all this going on. "Wow," they said. "That's really something. I'll bet if we used the name of Jesus the way Paul does, we could do that, too. Let's try it out." So they went into a house where there was a man that everybody thought was possessed by one of those evil spirits because he was acting very strangely. The seven brothers gathered around him and said with confidence: "In the name of the Jesus whom Paul talks about, come out!"

It didn't happen the way they were expecting. Instead of the evil spirit saying "OK, you've got me. I'm leaving," it said: "I know who Jesus is, and I know who Paul is, and I will obey them. But WHO ARE YOU? I don't have to do anything you say!" The evil spirit rose up and started hitting them and beating on them so much that all seven of the brothers ran out of the house as fast as they could, full of cuts and bruises.

You can imagine what all the neighbors thought. They figured that anybody who didn't take Jesus' power seriously, and Paul's power, too, as the representative of Jesus, could get in really big trouble. They decided that following Jesus was the smart thing to do, so they started singing the praises of Jesus and believing in him. Before this, they had depended a lot on magical formulas that they collected in books to tell them how to act and what to believe.

Do you like bonfires? You would have been happy to be there at the end of the story. The people took all their books about magic and burned them in a big fire. Paul and his friends joined in and had lots of fun. Maybe they even toasted marshmallows, except that we're really not sure if they had marshmallows that long ago.

Acts 19:11–20

CPSIA information can be obtained
at www.ICGtesting.com
Printed in the USA
FSHW020700210421
80524FS